THE
POWER
—OF YOUR—
VOTE

*Look past theatrics,
Assess your priorities, and
Make educated choices*

MARIE-AGNÈS PILON

THE POWER
—OF YOUR—
VOTE

THE
POWER
—OF YOUR—
VOTE

*Look past theatrics,
Assess your priorities, and
Make educated choices*

MARIE-AGNÈS PILON

AUTHOR ACADEMY elite

Copyright © 2019 Marie-Agnès Pilon. All right reserved.

Printed in the United States of America

Published by Author Academy Elite
P.O. Box 43, Powell. OH 43035
www.AuthorAcademyElite.com

All rights reserved. This book contains material protected under International and Federal Copyright Laws and Treaties. Any unauthorized reprint or use of this material is prohibited. No part of this book may be reproduced or transmitted in any form or by any means, electronic or mechanical, including photocopying, recording, or by any information storage and retrieval system, without express written permission from the author.

Identifiers:
LCCN: 2019915277
ISBN: 978-1-64085-969-2 (paperback)
ISBN: 978-1-64085-970-8 (hardback)
ISBN: 978-1-64085-971-5 (ebook)
Available in paperback, hardback, and e-book.

Any Internet addresses (websites, blogs, etc.) and telephone numbers printed in this book are offered as a resource. They are not intended in any way to be or imply an endorsement by Author Academy Elite, nor does Author Academy Elite vouch for the content of these sites and numbers for the life of this book.

DEDICATION

I dedicate this to all the voters that reach the point of confusion yet manage to still vote. To all the courageous people protesting, signing petitions, and engaging with politicians and policy makers. To people who ensure that politicians remember they are employed by the voters, not the lobbyists, not the party members, and not the people who donate money to their parties. To Canadian citizens who vote and engage in the democratic process, this is for you.

To the next generations, the current generations, and the generations to come who will participate in democracy and elections, this is for you.

CONTENT

Introduction: There is Power in Voting   1

PART I: WHAT'S IN THE MESSAGE?

Chapter 1: Political Spectrum   7
Chapter 2: Agenda, Bias, and Propaganda   11
    Agenda   12
    Bias   13
    Propaganda   15
Chapter 3: Opinion, Perception, and Perspective   18
    Opinion   19
    Perception   20
    Perspective   21
Chapter 4: The Medium of Emotions   25

PART II: SOURCES AND RESOURCES

Chapter 5: Elections Resources   33

Chapter 6: Sources	38
Partisan Sources and Information	39
Traditional Media	40
Social Media	42
Chapter 7: The Myths	46
Lowering taxes will put more money in the pocket of electors	46
Promising to cancel contracts costs nothing	49
Politicians with no experience should not govern	50
Politicians are all the same	51
People do not lie on the internet	52
Politicians are expert at politics	54
Saving the environment will cost our economy	54
My vote will not make a difference	56

PART III: YOUR PRIORITIES, YOUR PERSPECTIVES, YOUR STRATEGIES

Chapter 8: It Starts with You	65
Chapter 9: Interviewing the Candidates	68
Chapter 10: Promises, Promises	72
Chapter 11: Let the Debate Begin	76

PART IV: CHOICES AND VOTING

Chapter 12: Making a Choice	83
Chapter 13: Voting Time!	85
Afterword: Democracy starts with a vote but does not end there	89
References	93
Index	97
About the Author	105

LIST OF ILLUSTRATIONS

Figure 1 - Political Spectrum 7

Figure 2 - 2015 Federal Election Results 58

Figure 3 - 2015 Federal Election with non-voters . . . 58

Figure 4 - 2011 Federal Election Results 59

Figure 5 - 2011 Federal Election with non-voters . . . 59

Figure 6 - 2008 Federal Election Results 60

Figure 7 - 2008 Federal Election with non-voters . . . 60

LIST OF ABBREVIATIONS

AB: Province of Alberta

AI: Artificial Intelligence

BBC: British Broadcasting Company

BC: Province of British-Columbia

Bloc: Bloc Quebecois party (also BQ)

CBC: Canadian Broadcasting Company

CRTC: Canadian Radio-Television and Telecommunication Commission

GP: Green Party of Canada and different provinces

MB: Province of Manitoba

NB: Province of New Brunswick

NL: Province of Newfoundland and Labrador

NS: Province of Nova Scotia

NWT: Northwest Territories

NAFTA: North American Free Trade Agreement

MP: Member of Parliament (Federal)

MPP: Member of Provincial Parliament

PEI: Province of Prince Edward Island

PM: Prime Minister of Canada

NDP: New Democratic Party (of Canada and each province)

PC: Progressive Conservative Party

QC: Province of Québec

SK: Province of Saskatchewan

YK: Yukon territories

WWI: World War one

WWII: World War two

ACKNOWLEDGMENTS

Thank you to all the generations before me that fought to ensure all Canadian citizens get the right to vote and the freedom to do so without interference. Thank you to my mom and dad they inspired me to make my own mind about who to vote for.

INTRODUCTION
THERE IS POWER IN VOTING

I remember the election of 1984 for two reasons. First, it was held on my 16th birthday. Second, the Progressive Conservative of Brian Mulroney won a majority to govern in Canada. I voted in my first election in 1988. I was 20 years old and it was all about the North American Free Trade Agreement (NAFTA). I remember almost nothing about the campaign itself. A friend who was studying economics at University was told by one of the professors that it was a good thing to vote for the NAFTA agreement. I remember who I voted for, but I am not going to say because it does not matter. What matters is that I have participated in all Federal and Provincial Elections ever since, even when I was not 100% sure who I was going to vote for until I was facing the ballot in front of me.

What has kept me on track is the realisation that elections are about imparting the power to citizen's representatives to govern a country, province, and municipality.

People of all walks of life would say that an election is about jobs, health care, the environment, or education. Those are issues that may be discussed and debated during the election campaign. Issues drive the government to decide what investment should be or shouldn't be made. Political parties will try to say exactly the right things about those issues so that you will vote for them. However, no matter what they say, it is really all about power. It is why politicians use the medium of emotions to influence public opinion to win elections.

The hard part for voters is to sift through all the messages and emotions in order to know to whom to give the power to govern for the next four years in Canada. That is such an important fact to remember: *it is not forever*. Your vote gives the power to govern for *four years at a time*. Your membership in a political party should not be a guarantee that you will give the party's candidate your vote. Campaigns should give the voters the real picture of what political parties and candidates plan to do with the power to govern.

Some politicians and media have talked about running a "clean" or "dirty" campaign. A clean campaign is when the message is about the issues, the facts, and the record of action. A dirty campaign means the attacks are more personal in nature, focused on the character of the candidates, often using out of context quotes that are wrapped up in a narrative to make the person look bad in every possible way. The dirty campaign will not tell you what the party or leader of the party will do if elected, but it can tell you a lot about their values and ethics. Clean or dirty, the point of view will affect commercials, ads, and public speaking engagements. In the end, the voter still needs to make a choice.

Voters must remember that every vote counts long after Election Day. To achieve this, more people need to vote and not simply give their vote to a party. Every job out there has accountability. The same is true for a Member of Parliament (MP) or Prime Minister (PM). Before being accountable to their political party, they are accountable to citizens of their region or riding. I am not a member of any political party because I believe that not one political party or one person has the solution to make Canada - or any province in the country - a better place for all. The disadvantage is that I do not have a vote or say to what a party puts in their program, chart, or candidate they put on their ballot.

There is always more than one way to participate in democracy. No matter where you choose to start, it always will end with voting at election time. The path you choose to take in your active participation in democracy and voting can be similar to mine. You might not become a member of a party, but you can actively vote and monitor government actions and politician communications. Or, you may choose to join a party, participate to create a campaign agenda, and vote on priorities for the party's platform. Even if you have a membership card to a political party, this book can still help you decide who to vote for and get to know the candidate in your riding. If political parties see a member card as a guaranteed vote, we need to change that.

Democracy requires voters to be informed, make a choice to participate, and vote. Without that vote, you give up your power to hold all levels of government accountable. Governments, once elected, are to work for all voters, even those that didn't vote for them as well as those that did not vote at all.

The book is separated into four sections that will go from the message of the candidate or the party to your final decision and voting. Part one will look at the message; what constitutes it, and what influences your understanding of the message. In the second part of the book, I give you some resources to understand how an election works. In part three, I ask questions to help you establish your priorities and needs. This will help you "interview" candidates by watching the debate as an interview. I will show you how to interpret the different promises politicians express during political campaigns. In part four, I will provide tools to make a choice and then go and vote.

Politics is about power and power only. Of course, people want to change things and make things better. However, when you go the political route, it is power that is sought after. Once a person gets elected, they get the ability to impose their views, solutions, and beliefs on an entire country or province. Voting is your power to choose a candidate that influences the path for the Federal, Provincial, and Municipal governments. The more citizens vote, the better politicians will remember that the way they will get elected is by speaking to all voters, not only the members of their parties or the lobbyists.

Your vote is precious. It is power - your power.

PART I
WHAT'S IN THE MESSAGE?

CHAPTER 1
POLITICAL SPECTRUM

Before we start analysing the message, let's look at its content, what influences its production, and its reception. The figure below shows the political spectrum of philosophy which is useful to understand the agenda and bias of political parties.

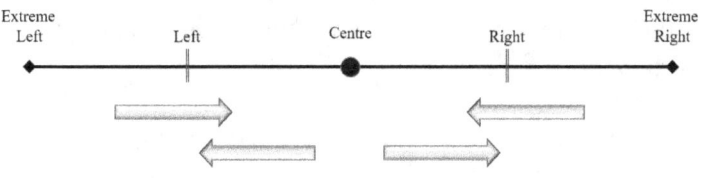

Figure 1 - Political Spectrum

As you can see, both right and left have extremes. You can imagine that anyone at the extreme spectrum may view the centre as an extreme. This figure is a way to visualise the different party's philosophies that will influence their message as each place on the spectrum has its bias, agenda, and propaganda. The most important aspect to remember is no political party remains stagnant in the spectrum. Think of the parties as a pendulum that swings back and forth in hopes to capture as broad of an audience as possible.

Socialism is considered to be on the left of the spectrum as it advocates government programs for all, like the health care system in Canada. Communism could be seen as the extreme left where everything is owned by the government or the community. Capitalism, which sits on the right of the spectrum, is a complete opposite to communism. One could surmise that capitalism is the extreme right, though it is not really thought of in that way.

Canada is a socio-capitalist political system. Individuals can own properties and companies. Government supplies services like schools, health care, unemployment benefits, old age benefits, and roads and transit paid for by the taxes collected on all Canadians. The different levels of government in Canada also own land, buildings, and corporations, often referred to as Crown Corporations. Even though the United States is thought of as only a capitalist system, there are numerous services provided by the government, such as unemployment insurance and the Federal highway system, both funded in the same way.

In Canada, the Conservative Party, or the variations of conservative parties, has been identified with the right as they prefer to have less government involvement and services. The Liberal Party usually is between the left and the centre of the spectrum as they support governmental programs, but it will restrict spending to appeal to members that are more to the right of the spectrum. The New Democratic Party (NDP) is a left wing party as they believe governments can do more to help the population have a better life however, they are far from being communist. As for the Green Party, it is a little harder to put them on the spectrum. The Green Party has economic strategies that differs from the other well-known parties. One of the guiding principle of The Green Party is to protect the environment to look for a more sustainable economic development.

There are many other political parties in Canada. You will need to do some research to know where they are on the political spectrum. Some of the political parties have websites that are accessible at all times however, others will have their websites up only during election time.

There are third party organisations that will also produce commercials and propaganda during election time. These parties may run campaigns at other times if they see something the government is doing they do not agree with. These organisations will also place themselves on the political spectrum that will support their philosophies, what they will advocate for, and against. It is a good idea to research them as they have become a part of the elections campaigns landscape.

If you are not sure where you are personally on this political spectrum, you may want to explore in depth what is left and right wing politics. Use the internet search. You will find a number of quizzes that can help you understand where you stand on the political spectrum. Remember to keep in mind each country may have a slight different take on the right and left wing politics or how the extreme of each side sits on the spectrum. Check to see if the website you are using for the quiz is in Canada.

Do not worry. You do not need to know if you are left, right, or more in the middle of the political spectrum to make a choice during an election. At times, these labels can feel like they do not match how you describe your political philosophy and what you consider a good government. Don't focus too much about the right or the left. Concentrate on finding a match between your priorities and the priorities of a political party's program.

CHAPTER 2
AGENDA, BIAS, AND PROPAGANDA

With words you can say anything. The expression "a picture is worth a thousand words" is from the point of view of the audience, not the artist. There are a lot of terms and turn of phrases when it comes to politics and political communication. No matter where the political parties or candidates are on the political spectrum, *agenda, bias, and propaganda* are the tools they use to construct their message and choose their words. These tools are how political communication is built, influenced, and massaged to reach its end goal: to persuade voters to vote for them. This is why, you the voter, need to understand those concepts and use them to decipher the message.

Words have different meanings depending of the context. When you are not sure what a word means or how the context in which it is used influence its meaning, reach for a dictionary. Dictionaries are a great starting point and a vetted source. Once you have the official definition, take a moment and make the word your own. You can do that by coming up with examples of what the word means to you or define it in your own words. By doing this, the meaning and its context will be your own. If someone challenges your interpretation of the word, you will have your own references and will be able to explain why you use the word the way you do.

Agenda

You will definitely hear this word tossed around during an election. It has many meanings and functions. We all have an agenda either in our personal life or at work. We all want to accomplish tasks and attain goals. We set ourselves an agenda to get there. It is a path that guides us to what we need to accomplish and what needs to happen for that goal to be achieved.

An agenda is also what political parties and candidates have when they set their party's political program. An agenda is used to construct their commercials. It determines what issues they bring to the forefront during debates or interviews. That is a political agenda.

The number one agenda of any political candidate or political party is to get your vote and gain the power to govern. When you listen to any election related communication, think about what influences the message. Apart from their own beliefs, bias, and experiences, *it is their agenda to get elected* and gain power to govern.

My agenda for this book is to get you to learn how to make an educated choice and to go vote. My intent is not to tell you who to vote for but to help you develop your own agenda, cast a vote, to choose who you want to govern your country, your province, and your municipality.

It is also important to inquire into a candidate's agenda which may correspond with the party or may differ from the party. A political candidate may also have some personal agenda. The only way to find this out is to do some research. Get to know your candidate better. See what agenda they have and how this agenda will influence how they will govern.

No matter who your candidate is, you will also want to get to know the agenda of the leader of the party. In Canada, at the Federal and Provincial level, the leader of the party with the most seats gets to be Prime Minister or Premier. That means you also need to be aware of the agenda of the party leader. Depending on what kind of leader they are, it is possible that the leader's agenda will override all other parties' agenda. This is where interviewing candidates and leaders comes into play.

Bias

Bias is a little tricky to make perfectly clear. Like an agenda, we all have biases. Biases influence the way we see the world, our assumptions about how the world works, and how we see people. Biases influence how we interact with each other, how we speak about a subject, or who we are likely to believe. Bias gets created by our experiences and the information we are exposed to from the media, school, friends, and family. Bias can prevent us from being open to new information or ideas. When biases interfere with absorbing new information or points of view, it can create distortion.

Politicians have biases to their own party programs and to whom they believe would vote for them. They also have personal biases exactly as you and I. It is important to understand that some of the biases spoken by a political candidate may not be their own. This is because the content of the campaign communication could be dictated by the party itself as a gatekeeper to what information should be shared with voters.

Sometimes, biases are used to influence the discourse of political parties or third parties. This can colour certain persons or situations to the point of exclusion. It can also feed propaganda in the hopes that voters will take on the bias. When a voter does this, they view the world through the perspective of the political party or candidate. This may, at the extreme, make voters view parts of the population as "undesirable" or "without needs".

Bias can also create blind spots. Blind spots are often created by propaganda or ideology that portrays some actions or spoken words as "common sense". Politicians also use blind spots and so-called common sense to reinforce certain bias to connect with voters and convince them to vote for what is presented as reflecting the same beliefs and image.

The best thing you can do about your biases is to be aware of them. That will help you see how they affect your perception of any messages or situations. It is important to understand our own biases as they can lead to prejudice towards candidates or ideas. Bias could make us miss important parts of messages as we would only focus on what resonates with what we know or think we know.

Propaganda

Propaganda is a word that seems to lose its meaning mainly because it is overused, although it is very real. I am not interested in scaring you. Like bias and agenda, the best thing to do about propaganda is to be aware of its existence. It is also important to remind ourselves that emotionally charged communications need to be taken with a grain of salt, especially if they are repeated over and over again.

Propaganda is used by all political parties and third parties alike to influence your vote. Most propaganda does not leave space for questions. It goes straight for your emotions, even if it is wrapped with some logic, statistics, and facts. All the information is aimed at getting a strong emotional reaction that will make you take a specific action that is in line with a specific goal. It is not necessarily the action that you would choose if you were calm, cool, and collected.

Propaganda will often point a finger at a reason why an event is happening or not happening. It wants to blind you to a single focal point and nothing else. It even will give you the "perfect" solution, pointing at a scapegoat to receive all the blame. Propaganda has an easy solution: simply remove the scapegoat. When its message gives you that kind of easy solution to a complex problem, you need to pause and investigate the whole situation. The other propaganda trick in commercials or political campaign messages is to pit X against Y. Take the time to ponder why you need to pick a side instead of finding a beneficial long lasting solution.

If you are listening to a commercial, interview, speech, or debate and you find yourself super emotional, for example:

very angry, full of fear or any other charged emotions, you are listening to propaganda. Stop for a moment. Breathe and delay any actions. Remove yourself from the situation. Think of why the message stirred so much emotion in you and in others. Again, this is not what the person selling the propaganda wants you to do. They want you to stay emotionally charged.

Propaganda has been used in the past during WWI and WWII by both sides of the war. Propaganda is a message that is repeated over and over in the hopes to become the only voice about a subject or point of view. This is another great incentive to have multiple sources of information. Get as many sources of information as possible so you can compare the propaganda messages, the facts, the statistics, and the points of view.

Candidates use various kinds of political vocabulary to build their message and exploit the political spectrum. However they all have an agenda, a bias, and use propaganda. If you focus on the agenda, the bias, and the propaganda, you will better understand what influences the content of the message.

Take the time to write down the words and definitions of any other terms used by the different political parties. Choose terms that puzzle you and look up their definitions in a dictionary. Then, take time to look at how they would influence the agenda, show a bias, and could shape propaganda. Don't forget to check all possible meanings of each word and how content and situation can change that meaning. If you want to have more information than you can digest, Google the word to see what pops up!

Questions to start your process:

- What influences you when it comes to democracy and politics?
- What are your political biases?
- What are you prone to believe at face value?
- What subject do you completely ignore or turn off when it comes up in discussions, commercials, or debate?
- Can you remember a commercial or slogan that made you feel something intensely?

CHAPTER 3
OPINION, PERCEPTION, AND PERSPECTIVE

Bias and agenda will inform the construction of the message with a specific point of view about an issue or a subject. Propaganda, with its method of repetition, frames it in a way that will promote a specific one-size-fits-all solution or a binary X vs. Y attitude most of the time. As an audience, you will have opinions and perceptions. With time and experience, you will gain perspective on the issues or subjects. Political parties and politicians have communication teams that prepare their messages to paint a picture that you, the audience, will perceive to produce an opinion.

Opinion

Our opinions are how we internally structure our understanding of an issue and how we construct where we stand on a subject, what we believe about the subject, and how we convey the subject to others. Opinions can be based on facts, experiences, first level encounter, and hand me down beliefs.

Some opinions may not even be our own. Sometimes, we adhere to someone else's view point, like an expert on the subject or a family tradition. We can take the opinions expressed by our circle of friends. Sometimes we do agree, other times we simply don't want to rock the boat. When we think about or talk about political opinion, there is always passion and distortion involved. We often form political opinions from what we hear and sometimes what we personally experience.

Our opinions are based on our perception of the world around us. There is a great way to make sure your opinion is your own: go to the source. When it comes to politics, try to get as close to the source of the message. To know what a candidate in your riding promises or says, go hear them speak or listen to a recorded speech. Ask questions directly to the candidate or the leader of any political party. After you've heard straight from the source, you can see how the media or experts analyze the information. Then, when you look at what others think or listen to their opinions, you will be able to compare it with your own information and expand your knowledge on the subject.

Perception

Perception is how you perceive and construct your experience of an event, commercial, speech, etc. It is the first impression you get when you meet someone new. However, we can get a second, third, or fourth impression also. Perceptions are not without distortions. What can distort your perception? It could be as simple as how you feel that day. It could also be as ingrained as your bias and your agenda.

Your personal bias and agenda will make you focus or look for specific content and information. This directs your attention and opens you up for information and communication that echoes, reinforces, and expands on what you know and how you feel about what you know. I think this is especially true when it comes to political parties and politicians.

People who do surveys, during election time and throughout the four year term, look to find out your perception of a campaign, a policy, and political party leaders. They will also try to gauge your opinions on the different issues. For example, different level of government will gauge how you perceive a new law or policy, and at the same time get your opinion on the environment or the economy.

Perceptions and opinions go hand in hand. Perceptions fuel the knowledge that we use to forge an opinion on anything and everything. When it comes to politics, our perception of the role of government, the value of the job of the members of parliament, and the election campaign can create some strong opinions spiced up by emotions stirred by the content of the political messages.

Perspective

Hindsight is 20/20 because it is easier to see with clarity after the fact. When you are in the middle of the action, you do not see everything around you, nor do you have multiple views of the situation. Perspective is similar to hindsight as you gain it by changing your point of view of a situation from your own perception to someone else's. Perspective is also gained over time. For example, if you were to revisit a house you lived in as a young child, you would notice that something you perceived as big is now only normal size. Another way to gain perspective is through accumulated experiences. You reflect back on how your perception of a situation or subject evolved with the knowledge you gain from your experiences.

Have you had anyone say to you that you are too close to something and you need to gain perspective? That usually happens when you are invested in a situation and there is a need to mentally or emotionally step back to see the larger picture. Often when we are invested in a situation, we can get tunnel vision, which matches our personal perceptions and opinions. In politics, we all get tunnel vision and rarely get a real perspective on the issues and solutions that are proposed by the different political parties.

Perspective is definitely needed when we are experiencing an election. Political parties and politicians will try to give a single point of view on an issue while framing other points of view as false, unnecessary, or distortions of the truth. At times, it feels like the commercials and messages are designed so you cannot even see any other point of view. This is usually accomplished by using vocabulary that is emotionally charged (see the medium of emotions).

Propaganda is a pesky tool to narrow the points of view. Since propaganda is constructed to either give a single possible solution or an X point of view vs. a Y point of view, you are often left without the big picture and simply have a few details of a complex situation. The only way to gain perspective is to make an effort to actively look for different points of view and opinions on any given situation or issue. This takes effort from us, the voters.

Perspective may not change your opinion or your perception. You will know where it fits in the grander scheme of things. It will enable you to speak your opinion with a little less emotion, more insight, and empathy. When you have perspective, you have empathy without changing your opinions or perceptions.

When it comes to government, it can be hard to gain a perspective when political parties, third parties, and political candidates' agendas are designed to get you, the voters, to see a situation from their point of view. They want you to buy-in to their vision of government involvement, social programs, foreign policies, environment policies, and economic development. It does take time and work to get perspective on those important subjects. We can all do it by taking the time to open our minds to more than one point of view, especially those with which we don't agree. Understanding why others have differing opinions is a valuable tool to gain perspective.

One way to have a good political perspective is to have a *political memory* (or memories). Often after four years (or more) of the current political party in power, we forget what it was like when the previous political party was in power. With old events not being in the news and previous Prime Minister no longer in politics, we forget the flaws or costly mistakes of former governments. Political parties vying for power will make sure that you only focus on the now. With voters having political amnesia, past mistakes or habits are out of view. Remember, perspective is a way to see the big picture and be able to understand how the details fit in it.

Often, journalist do a retrospective of previous governments with a comparison to the current government. With social media, you will also find people posting information about the current and previous government. Take the information, *verify it*, and gain perspective to expand your perceptions. This will help you build new opinions or reinforce the opinions you already have.

Questions:

- What is your perception of power?
- What is your perception and opinion on the Federal/Provincial government involvement in: Economic, Environment, Social programs?
- What is your opinion on the different political parties in our country or in your province?
- What is your perception of the political party leaders?
- What opinion do you think is not your own about politicians or political party?

CHAPTER 4
THE MEDIUM OF EMOTIONS

McLuhan coined the phrase "The medium is the message". For politics, the medium is emotions, even when mixed with statistics and facts. Emotions create strong reactions from the audience of voters. It is often the type of reaction propaganda attempts to create. It is important to remind voters to watch how political messages play with their emotions. Playing with people's emotions is a deceitful way to make voters overlook what is not said or what could be implied by the message or the medium.

In 1964, Marshall McLuhan stated " What matters is the medium, not the message, because the message of any medium or technology is the change of scale or pace or pattern that it introduces into human affairs." (Laughey 2007) In other words, the messages contained in any medium are inseparable from the medium's human consequences, and it is these consequences that matter most. Therefore, "the medium is the message because it is the medium that shapes and controls the scale and form of human association and action" (Laughey 2007). For example, television's medium is the images it broadcast more than the words that are spoken to accompany the images. The images are what stay with the audience.

Why do I say the medium of political messages is emotion? If you think about it, most political advertisement, speech, or debate have statistics and facts wrapped up in emotions. This is a small extrapolation of what a medium is as thought of by McLuhan. It expresses how often political candidates and parties use the emotions of fear, anger, loyalty, and belonging. Their agenda is to get people to vote for them, or more appropriately, not to vote for the other parties.

What are the human consequences of using the medium of emotion to gain power?

It can create division. It clouds judgement on the consequence of the vote. It also clouds the intentions of the candidates and the parties involved in the medium of emotion. When a message strikes certain emotional chords, like fear or anger, it prevents the receiver from having a real perspective on the issue. Emotions don't know how to make sense of the statement or the facts that are poured through commercials, newspaper articles, speeches, and social media.

As voters, we need to remind ourselves that what candidates want is the power to govern. Emotions are normal every day occurrences. Political messages that focuses on getting certain emotions revved up, like fear and anger, create a distortion of the perception of the information in the message. If a commercial or social media message really gets your emotions revved up, take a step back and pause for a moment. Before, reposting or responding, take stock of your emotions. Ask yourself: What in the message really got to me? Why did it get to me? What's the purpose of using this emotion to portray the issue or candidate?

Political parties and candidates will say whatever it takes to get people to go out and vote. They will use polls and research to gather information about what voters are unhappy about; what they want the government to do or not do, etc. With that, they craft a message with facts, statistics, and information coupled with emotionally charged words. The goal is for voters to only remember the emotion, not the information. However, emotions can overwhelm and confuse voters to the point of feeling like they cannot make a real decision. That is another strategy. Political parties at times may use the medium of emotions to ensure voters will *stay home* on Election Day.

Political parties, special interest groups, and candidates use and abuse the medium of emotion. Their goal is still to gain power by getting voters to choose them. It is the hard job of the voter to sift through the misinformation and emotional distractions to get to the information. Part of this investigation also requires voters to ask: why are they using fear or anger as the medium for their message? Why are they doing a character assassination?

Sometimes campaigns are described as dirty or clean depending on whether the message emphasis is about smearing the opponent or talking about the party's program and goals once in office. I would add that if a political party uses the emotions of fear and anger as the medium of their message, the campaign is also a dirty campaign. Why? Simply because fear and anger are not emotions that inspire trust when it is used to gain power. And an election is about power.

As a voter, I do need to be informed about the risks and rewards involved in the program of any given political party. If a political party wins the election, there is no guarantee that they will follow their program. I get confused when all I am left with is emotion. Sometimes the message is wrapped in positive emotion and intention. I listen when politician talk about their program positively and enthusiasm without bashing any other program or part of society. I feel like I am getting informed about the plan of the political party and the candidate's plan. I can then assess what they are proposing and decide if what they propose matches my priorities.

Political parties do have a choice when they use the medium of emotions. At times, they may even strive for a more neutral language. As long as they talk about their own projects, positions, and vision for the next four years. However, when they simply keep dramatizing the other political parties' program, they do not inform the voters about what will happen if they are elected. It simply becomes theatrics.

What history has taught me is that no government has a perfect record. No governments elected in Canada were mistake free. No Canadian Federal or Provincial Government can control what will happen over the four year term in power.

I have often felt confusion when a message tries to scare me away from voting for one candidate or if the message tries to pit me against another part of the population. The best thing I have done is to listen to my emotions and ask, why do they want me to feel this way? What would happen if I give power to this political party or candidate?

The medium of emotion is often found in vocabulary and intonation. Emotions are also attached to social status, needs, and wants. Take the time to pay attention to the words, the intention, and voice used by the candidates, political parties, and special interest parties. They all want either the power to govern or prevent someone from getting the power to govern. Make sure the medium of emotion does not prevent you from voting.

Questions:

- What are words used in political slogans that you would categorize as negative, positive, or neutral?
- Does the message feel like it is dividing or rallying?
- Do you feel informed or emotional after listening to a commercial, speech, or debate?

PART II
SOURCES AND RESOURCES

CHAPTER 5
ELECTIONS RESOURCES

At times it feels like those in charge of an election, the regulation body, are far away and unreachable. That is not the case. Election Canada, as well as the Provincial counterpart, is available to all Canadian citizens. Election Canada is the branch of government that runs, monitors, and regulates political campaigns. It registers voters, candidates, and political parties as well as third parties or special interest parties. This information is important when trying to understand an election. I will not restate what is already on the website. Instead, I will share how you can get in contact with them. The electoral regulating bodies for the Federal and Provincial elections have a lot of information about elections, and are real entities that voters need to get to know.

Election Canada is for all information about Federal Elections.

- Websites: http://www.elections.ca/home.aspx.
- Twitter account: @ElectionsCan_E (English), @Electionsan_F (French).
- Facebook page: https://www.facebook.com/ElectionsCanE (English), https://www.facebook.com/ElectionsCanF (French).
- YouTube channel: https://www.youtube.com/c/ElectionsCanadaE (English), https://www.youtube.com/c/ElectionsCanadaF (French).
- LinkedIn page: https://www.linkedin.com/company/elections-canada/ (bilingual page).
- Instagram account: https://www.instagram.com/electionscan_e/ (English), https://www.instagram.com/electionscan_f/ (French).
- If you are not internet savvy or would prefer to talk to some, you can reach them by phone at 1-800-463-6868.
- Email address: info@elections.ca

Election Canada has all the information a voter needs to know about elections. Their mission is to ensure "that Canadians can exercise their democratic rights to vote and be a candidate" (Election Canada 2019). Election Canada is responsible for Federal general elections. You can find a complete list of candidates in previous Federal elections as well as the current election. They also have statistics on voter turnout from 1867 to 2015. The website also has links to the "History of Federal Riding" since 1867, which list the candidates, total votes for each, their profession, and who was elected.

Election Canada also has an educational section to help voters learn about elections and give school teachers tools to teach their students about elections. Election Canada lists all the Federal political parties in Canada, which is updated when "written reports are generated and signed by the leader of the party" (Election Canada 2019). Each time a new leader of a political party reports to Election Canada to register their political party, this information is updated.

There are Provincial electoral entities that perform the same duties as the Federal electoral entity. Here is a list of each with their website and phone numbers in alphabetical order of province name.

Alberta
Website: www.elections.ab.ca
Phone number: 1-780-427-7191
Email Address: info@elections.ab.ca

British Columbia
Website: www.elections.bc.ca
Phone number: 1-800-661-8683
Email Address: electionsbc@elections.bc.ca

Manitoba
Website: www.electionsmanitoba.ca
Phone number: 1-866-628-6837
Email Address: election@elections.mb.ca

New Brunswick
Website: www.electionsnb.ca
Phone number: 1-800-308-2922
Email Address: info@electionsnb.ca

Newfoundland & Labrador
Website: www.elections.gov.nl.ca/elections/
Phone number: 1-877-729-7987
Email Address: enl@gov.nl.ca

Northwest Territories
Website: www.electionsnwt.ca
Phone number: 1-844-767-9100
Email Address: info@electionsnwt.ca

Nova Scotia
Website: www.electionsnovascotia.ca
Phone number: 1-800-565-1504
Email Address: elections@novascotia.ca

Nunavut
Website: www.elections.nu.ca
Phone number: 1-800-267-4394
Email Address: info@elections.nu.ca

Ontario
Website: www.elections.on.ca
Phone number: 1-888-668-8683
Email Address: info@elections.on.ca

Prince Edward Island (PEI)
Website: www.electionspei.ca
Phone number: 1-888234-8683
Email Address: info@electionspei.ca

Québec
Website: www.electionsquebec.qc.ca
Phone number: 1-888-353-2846
Email Address: info@electionsquebec.qc.ca

Saskatchewan
Website: www.elections.sk.ca
Phone number: 1-877-958-8683
Email Address: info@elections.sk.ca

Yukon
Website: www.electionsyk.ca
Phone number: 1-866-668-8683
Email Address: info@electionsyukon.ca

These websites and organisations are there for voters to obtain information about political parties, candidates, statistics, and political donations. Get yourself familiar with them as it also contains a number of reports about each election. The Federal and Provincial electoral bodies will serve you in French and English at a minimum.

CHAPTER 6
SOURCES

You need to have multiple sources. Information is only valuable when you know its source. Sometimes it is easier to go to the same source for all your information. If you do that, you will always get the same opinions, points of view, and perspective. Your perception will rely on the same understanding of an issue, situation, or ideas, resulting in a bit of tunnel vision. Reading or listening to multiple sources may enhance your understanding of what is happening and what is being done to deal with it. It will inform you of opposite points of view for sure. It may also inform you of the issues from a different angle giving you a different perspective. A different angle may not be its direct opposite. Real life is not simply binary.

Not one person has all the answers or all the information. Varying the source of your information may open yourself to new perspectives. It may not change your opinion or perception of an issue or subject. It will make you better informed. It will give you an understanding of where people may be coming from when they talk about the issue or subject.

We don't all have time to find the source of the information we are receiving. In a way, the traditional news media like television, radio, and newspapers were the ones tasked to find the source of the information being broadcasted. When it comes to social media, you may have to dig into the information yourself to find the "original" source of the message. Remember that when it comes to an election, it is about power. There are a lot of people who want that power to govern or to influence who governs and how they go about governing.

Partisan Sources and Information

When looking to understand what a party is planning to do if they are elected, the best place to go is their published platform. These platforms are normally published on the party's website. The best place to go to know how many parties there are in a Federal election and what candidates are in your electoral district is Election Canada. The same information is available on each province electoral body's website.

Usually, we hear about party platforms through the news, commercials, televised speech, regional events, and debates. Debates are a separate entity, mainly because the candidates are there to answer questions, not explain their platform. The different channels of communication will never give you the entire party platform. The website of each party will also give you more information about the history, beliefs, and governing documents of each political party. It will also give you the possibility to become a member and learn about the executive of the party.

The idea is not to understand everything, but to be aware of the different proposition by each party. This will help you and me when we interview the candidates and the party leaders (Chapter 8). It is also a great source of information when you compare your personal priorities (Chapter 7) with that of each party. This is getting information from the source.

There is also something called a third party. According to election Canada, "a third party is a person or group that conducts election advertising, other than a candidate, registered party or electoral district association." (Election Canada 2019) It is also important to know that "a foreign third party that is not eligible to register can spend only up to $499.99 on election advertising." (Election Canada 2019) Election Canada also has a list of registered third parties if you want to know more about them or if you saw a commercial from one of them. They can also spend money before the election campaign start as it is not considered election time.

It would be beneficial to know the background of the registered third parties as they also have bias, agendas, use propaganda, and definitely use the medium of emotion. Some of these third parties look at different aspects of election that may not be covered by the news or social media.

Traditional Media

Television, newspapers, radio online, and airways are still a great source of candidate profiles, background, and current campaign development as well as interviews of party leaders and candidates. This is a place to use when checking information found on social media or in the partisan channels.

Each region in Canada has local newspapers, although they are growing scarce. If you have them in your area, it is a great place to get information about the campaign, local candidate, and events like debates that will involve the person you will vote for.

Traditional media have licenses to broadcast and have to answer to complaints against what they do broadcast. The Canadian Radio-Television and Telecommunications Commission (CRTC) is the entity in Canada responsible for issuing the licenses and to monitor the use of that license. (CRTC 2019) In the traditional media, they are gatekeepers. Gatekeepers select what will be broadcast on the air, printed on paper, or published on their websites. These gatekeepers have their own bias and agenda as well as responsibilities. The gatekeepers usually answer to the owner of the television, radio, or newspapers. The owners of television stations, radio stations, and newspapers, have their own bias, opinions, and political allegiance.

Much of the traditional media will disclose the source of their information and be responsible to authenticate the information they broadcast. They will not reveal how certain stories get chosen for a broadcast while others are left off the air. With the digital age, traditional media will broadcast more stories on the internet. The cost for the space is less on a webpage then on a piece of paper. Online, there are no time limits like there is for a television news broadcast, which is normally one hour.

There are continuous news channels that usually concentrate on a few in-depth stories. They have a variety of shows for business news, international news, national, and provincial news. It gives a wider spectrum of news with special programming when news breaks or when a new budget is introduced at the Federal or Provincial level. They are all great sources of news and their websites give even more information.

With the traditional media, the journalists who cover the news and events have a responsibility to be as neutral as possible when constructing their stories. They are expected to contact all parties to give a complete overview of what happened, who was involved, where it happened, when it happened, how it happened, and if possible, why it happened. If what the journalist reports is incorrect, there are repercussions and the public can contact the network or newspaper the journalist works for.

Social Media

There is an incredible array of information from a multitude of sources available on the internet that depart from the traditional media such as blogs, Facebook posts, Twitter, Instagram, and other forms of social media. It really looks as if there are no gatekeepers, so all stories, perspectives, perceptions, and opinions freely flow from one person to the next.

The information shared creates new communities of like-minded individuals even if they are oceans apart. It helps to show more images, news, and daily activities from different parts of the world. It also makes some news stories available to all, without a gatekeeper or editor to structure the narrative. One example of this is the Arab Spring, where images from Cairo and other cities were made available to all from people participating or witnessing the events.

As the technology evolved and as more people subscribed to the different social media, political parties, third parties, and influencers[1] have flooded the gates with specific information and propaganda. Today there are known programs, like twitter bots that post messages for you without your knowledge. It is practical when you want to increase your online presence without having to be present online.

There are also fake accounts, built to flood the gates and push messages out to as many people as possible. Often, when we retweet or repost, we do not check the source or the veracity of the content. On social media, you may encounter messages that look like it's from a voter just like you, or posing as one, but it is in fact a party's social media feed. It is useful to do some digging to make sure you understand the agenda and bias behind the message. Sometimes, the message looks benign; however, it comes from an organization with a specific agenda. It becomes the responsibility of every user to verify what they are publishing to their own followers.

On social media, there are no journalist like on traditional media. Traditional media and journalists do have social media presence. However, the vast majority of the information comes from individuals, communities, or groups interacting with others, simply having a social exchange. Sometimes you may not have the resources to investigate where the messages are coming from. The

---

[1] Influencer is a person that has a platform to broadcast information. They have acquired a reputation for "being in the know" and either being factual about situation or honest and truthful. They also have gained influence by asserting themselves as a subject matter expert.

great thing is, you can follow a journalist or newsfeed from traditional media and ask them what they know. This is part of the social media experiment.

You can easily find people of like mind and mindset on the internet through social media. It is also easy to explore different ideas, perspectives, and knowledge. For elections, I would suggest following as many leaders of as many political parties as possible. You will then be able to see how they evolve and what they say directly on social media. Include the candidates in your riding in your social media feed. Local, national, and provincial content is important. By being exposed to what is close, and to what is farther away, you will get a perspective and may learn how other parts of the country or province view your region.

Remember, social media is about connecting. As much as party leaders often only post and do not reply, sometimes they are not even the ones typing the message. You can engage them. I would recommend being courteous and respectful, even if you do not agree with their messages. This engaging with political candidate and party leaders is a great way to give them feedback. Following them on social media will let you see comments and who agrees or disagrees with them.

Social media can also be overwhelming when people and programs flood the gates with similar messages over and over again. The different owners of the different social media applications like Facebook, Twitter, Instagram, and others, are working at being more vigilant about what is published on their platforms. Remember, just because something is retweeted, reposted, and shared by a lot of people does not necessarily make it true. The purpose of electronic propaganda is to flood the fields of information.

Be aware and question any emotionally charged communication. Elections are about power. Flooding the information field with subjects and opinions can influence the results of an election.

Always check the publishing date. This is important because at election time, people like to rehash old stories. They might not put out the entire story. Often times, they focus on the negative and not the resolution. It's unlikely they will publish corrections. The past is relevant to the present as it can help gain perspective and understand the evolution of a situation, a Member of Parliament, or a candidate. Every party and candidate have a past. Remember party members and candidates do change from one election to the next. Compare the past with the present before making judgements based only on the past.

CHAPTER 7
THE MYTHS

I want to talk about some of the myths about governing, promises, information, and solutions to our Federal or Provincial issues. For all of the myths that I can think about, I am sure you know some too. I did research on all of the myths below using the internet, making sure I had multiple sources. I educated myself about what I have heard over the years on television, radio, and read in a newspaper from political candidates and voters.

Lowering taxes will put more money in the pocket of electors

This has to be one of the favourite promises that politicians and candidates like to make. We will lower your taxes and you will have more money in your pocket. It is partially true that when taxes are lowered, we have more money in our pockets. It always depends on what tax they are lowering.

When lowering income taxes, we may get more money on every pay cheque depending on the tax bracket affected by the change and if you are in that tax bracket. Lowering sales tax helps consumers have greater buying power. What we need to buy will cost us less, although products classified as basic groceries already do not get taxed in Canada. Your grocery bill may not be reduced by lowering sales taxes though many items, like soap, clothing, and prepared foods will cost less with a tax reduction.

Politicians rarely speak about the cost of lowering taxes. When a government, Federal or Provincial, lowers taxes, they lower their revenues. The revenue from taxes is how the Federal and Provincial government get money to fund healthcare, education, road maintenance, etc. See the information below outlining some of the responsibilities of each level of government.

Federal Government: National Defence, Criminal Law, Employment Insurance, Postal Services, Census, Foreign Affairs, Banking, Federal Taxes, Income Tax, Fisheries, Shipping, Railways, Telephones, Pipelines, Indigenous Lands and Rights, Agriculture, Immigration, Healthcare (transfer of funding), Federal Prisons and Environment.

Provincial Government: Direct Taxes, Health Care, Prisons, Education, Marriage, Property and Civil Rights, Agriculture, Immigrations, Road Regulations, Administration of Justice, and Environment.

Municipal Government: Parks, Parking, Libraries, Roadways, Local Police, Local Land Use and Planning (zoning), Fire Protection, Public Transportation, Community Water System, Waste Collection, Emergencies Services, Animal Control, and Economic Development.

We also have to remember that the higher levels of government push down money to the lower levels of government. If the Federal government collects less money, there is less money to transfer to the Provincial government. That is not to say that a tax cut for consumers and workers is a bad thing, but it does have an impact on the services each level of government can provide to the entire population of Canada and each of its province and territories.

Let's do some simple math. According to Statistic Canada, in February of 2019 there were approximately 19,056,800 of people that were either full time or part time employees. (Statistics Canada 2019) If either the Federal or Provincial government change the taxes to reduce income tax on employees' paycheck by 1,000 dollars a year (to make the math simple). That is a loss of revenue of 19,056,800,000 dollars. Often not all workers, full time and part time, will get the full income tax reduction. However, the promise often does not state how they will replace the missing income.

Now it is true that some people will take the 1,000 dollars and put it back into the economy, and the Federal or Provincial government will get some of the amount back. However, that is a deficit that needs to be accounted for. This deficit is rarely (or never) talked about. Usually it means less services for the whole population. You need to ask yourself, is the government providing the services I need with the tax money they collect? And if everyone that gets the 1,000 dollars back puts it in a saving accounts for a rainy day, it may take a long time for the governments to see some revenue.

Promising to cancel contracts costs nothing

Over the years, new governments come in and cancel awarded contracts from the previous government because they believe it is not needed, it's too expensive, or they simply promised to do so. It is the right of a new government to cancel the previous government policies or contract, as stated in a Fraser Research Bulletin in October 2014. (Fraser Institute 2014)

The problem with continuously cancelling what has been done in the past four years is that you never get to go to something else. You keep working on the same things over and over again unless the same political party gets re-elected to govern for another four years.

Cancelling certain contracts, like defense contracts, do incur monetary penalties and probably job loss. A lot of contracts by the department of defense sometimes require that investment be made in Canada as part of what can be called a return on investment. I did a few searches on Google about cancelled contracts or delayed contracts. I found some interesting information, but most of it was from the Bryan Mulroney and Jean Chretien eras of cancelling the replacement of the Canadian Navy's helicopter. I also found the information that identifies the cost of one billion dollars if the Trudeau Liberal government were to cancel the contract to send light armoured vehicles to Saudi Arabia. (The Canadian Press 2018) (Urback 2018) (Chase 2018)

At times during political campaigns, the opposition vying for the power to govern will take to task a previously awarded contract by the current government. They do this because they see it as a way of gaining supporters and votes. They find numbers and facts that support their arguments and start repeating their message. They also promise to award a more beneficial contract for Canadians and Canadian industries if they are elected to power.

Often, their numbers and facts lack the information about the consequence of cancelling the contract. In the Fraser report, they talk about continuously cancelling contracts eventually "erodes confidence in doing business with government, and thus impairs the credit of the Crown and economic conditions in the jurisdiction." (Fraser Institute 2014)

The bigger problem is that as voters, we are not privy to all the workings of awarding and cancelling contacts for the Federal and Provincial government. We don't know if companies doing business with our government start asking for *higher cancellation fees* because of history repeating itself.

If, during an election, a political party proposes to cancel contracts or program, voters should ask what the cost of it will be. It may end up that canceling is the right thing to do, however we need to hear the pros and cons. Merely adding the word "savings" to a number the party has come up with is not the same as having all the facts.

Politicians with no experience should not govern

The interesting part of that myth is that even though some political parties have had a turn at governing, the current candidates may be inexperienced. Political parties change leaders from one election to the next, especially if party members are not happy with the results or if they lose confidence in their leader.

The political party organisation does have members that stay on for many years and can give advice on how it was done in the past and what is required. The civil servants also know what needs to be done and will guide a newly elected political party.

The decisions from the previous government and the dossier information stay with each ministry, so the new minister and cabinet members can review the information and get up to speed.

Will there be errors? Probably. Experience does not shield any elected official from mistakes. When you decide who to vote for, experience can be a factor. Perhaps what is most important is to have a proposed plan and to have the willingness to ask questions to ensure procedures are followed and respected. If we keep voting the same parties to govern and expect change to happen, that might be a very flawed premise. If you are not happy with how previous parties have governed the country or your province, maybe it is time to look at the other political parties.

Politicians are all the same

Sometimes it does feel like all politicians have the same type of behaviours, and when scandals occur, it is easy to put them all in the same basket and give up. I have friends who will not vote because they say politicians are all the same and their votes will not make a difference.

I believe politicians, political parties, and civil servants are different, though they all face the bureaucracy and legacy of the government rules, regulations, and procedures. There are pitfalls and temptations when someone is placed in a position of power. Governing a country or province is being in a position of power.

Elected officials want to do what is best for the country or provinces. They each have their ideas on how to get there. They also want to do some good for the riding that elected them. Remember, lobbyists are paid to get the attention of elected officials in hopes to get contracts or legislation to change rules and regulations to make it easier for them. As voters, we are busy with our lives. We do not have the time to keep knocking on the doors of members of parliament. But it would be nice to know that politicians remember who actually gave them the mandate to govern. The voters, not the lobbyists.

These pressures exist for any government or elected official. A number of ethics rules and officers have been put in place at the Federal and Provincial level to help elected officials in making the right decision. The ethics rules are there to remind elected officials that citizens, not corporations, vote to elect them.

People do not lie on the internet

People lie at times in real life, and people also lie on the internet. The harder part about the internet and social media is the verification of the information. It does not mean that everyone on social media or the internet lies. It means they are capable of lying. Your job is *not* to take everything you read on the internet at face value. Try to find the source of the information. Ask others on the internet or in your circle of friends what they think. Don't automatically share or pass on the information. Take the time to verify what is said. If you cannot figure out if it is true or not, don't pass it on. This is probably good advice even if you agree with some of the information in the message.

Another good practice is if you know the information is not accurate, or simply a lie, is to say so. Report it as a spam to the social media provider. The internet, like traditional media, will provide accurate information if we make sure we demand it.

With politics, what is on the internet may not be complete lies nor complete truths. Political parties and candidates are looking to say what will get voters to vote for them. Keep this in mind when a political party sends messages or commercials, and comes up with slogans. They may take statements out of context to make it fit or to discredit another political party or candidate.

You also need to be aware that there is new Artificial Intelligence (AI) programming that can be used to create fake audio and video that are hard to distinguish from reality. (Vincent 2017) (BBC 2017) I am not sure how this will play out in coming elections or how Election Canada will regulate these. Just be aware that there are more and more ways to create fake information on the internet. (Taulli 2019) (O'Sullivan 2019)

If you search long enough on the internet, you can find people that think exactly like you do. If you search long enough, you will find information that reinforces your beliefs. Numbers, pictures, and words can be made to imply almost anything. The question still remains: is it true, half-true, or made to look true. When it comes to influencing power and gaining power, some are willing to push their agenda before anything else.

Politicians are expert at politics

No, they are not. Actually, some of them are not expert in the type of ministry they manage. Some are expert in a field like law, medicine, or business. There is no required college degree to become a politician or candidate during an election. You do not even need experience in politics. Politicians, once elected, rely on experts in different fields when creating a new piece of legislation. It is important to know that governing is not like running a business. Every government needs to strive to balance their budget. They face some uncertainty and do not control the economies of other countries. Even experienced politicians make mistakes and face new situations.

Saving the environment will cost our economy

This is a true double edged sword! Without the environment, we do not have an economy, nor do we have a life outside of work. Most businesses depend on the environment to provide some of the resources needed to produce their products. Climate change creates the possibilities of destruction or damaging of those assets because of extreme weather events. The other risk is to our ability to have an environment we can live in comfortably and enjoy during after work hours.

Economists, scientists, businesspeople, and politicians warn us and try to reassure us. Government has to balance the need of businesses today with the needs of people today. They must see the need in twenty years for businesses and people working together. Governments are elected for four year terms. If they are lucky, they get a second term. That would mean they may get eight years to implement changes. Realistically, they have four years.

The answer: it is hard to make changes when you do not see the impact on the environment. So far, the climate changes have had minimal impact where I live. However, we have more droughts during the summer impacting the yield of crops. Less snow in the winter means that we need more rain in the spring to ensure the ground is wet enough to help seeds sprout.

One thing is for sure; care for the environment is not only up to the government or big companies. There has got to be a way to make money with a greener economy. The quicker we switch to that, the less our economy could be impacted with the climate changes. We need to understand how our day to day behaviour impacts the environment. That is a challenge. We also need to have some long-term vision about the economy and our environment. The consequences may not show up until ten to twenty years down the road. We can gradually make changes now, or we will be forced to make a massive, messy change of direction later.

Politicians are not experts and certainly not on the effect of climate change. Your vote can decide which way a government steers the "environment vs. economy" debate. Part of the truth is that you have no economy without an environment. Workers without a healthy environment, are not healthy productive workers for the big companies that produce the products we believe we cannot live without.

This is one topic you will have to research on your own. There is a lot of information out on the web including research papers and news articles. Some people say climate change is a hoax and it will pass. Maybe that is true, however, you need to look at multiple sources and make up your mind. The environment can impact life, the economy, and your finances directly and indirectly. Directly could be damage to your home or workplace. Indirectly could be damage in another country impacting the supply chain of goods and services you use and purchase. It can indirectly affect your retirement fund and your investments.

My vote will not make a difference

I have heard that excuse many times. The truth is, an election is won by a simple majority, 50% of the vote plus 1. One vote can win an election. Some elections have been won by as little as five or ten votes. Every vote matters. If more people voted, politicians would also pay more attention. It is important to understand that a majority of seats in parliament does not mean a majority of voters voted for the political party now governing for the next four years. Below you will find the last three Federal election statistic about voter turnout.

In the 2015 Federal election, the voter turnout was 68.3% (Election Canada 2019) that means a little more than 30% of eligible voters did not exercise their right to vote. In the 2011 Federal election the turnout was 61.1% (Election Canada 2019) and in 2008 it was 58.8% (Election Canada 2019). Let's explore how this 30 to 40% of extra voters could have made a difference. For ease of calculation, I will set the voter turnout for 2015 at 68%, 2011 at 61% and 2008 at 59%. The percentage of voters that did not vote is 32% in 2015, 39% in 2011 and 41% in 2008.

To explain my numbers, I took the election results of the number of seats and percentage of the vote by each party during the three elections. I prorated the percentage to include the percentage of people that did not vote. There is no calculable correlation between the percentages of vote to seat ratio. I will not estimate how many more seats a party could receive if the percentage of people that did not vote had voted. However, these figures are interesting to ponder. So the figures 7.1, 7.3, and 7.5 are the percentages based on 100% of the people that *actually voted*. (The Canada Guide 2017) Figures 7.2, 7.4, and 7.6 are based on 100% of *eligible voters*, so in 2008 the Conservatives received 38% of votes from those who voted. But only 22% of all eligible voters. (The Canada Guide 2017)

58   THE POWER OF YOUR VOTE

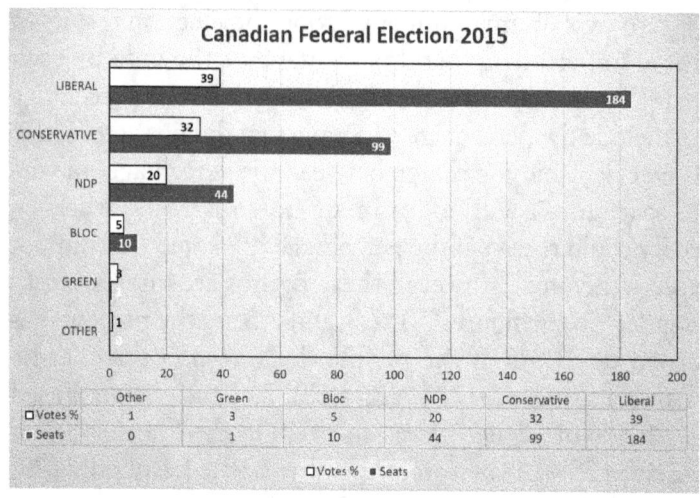

Figure 2 - 2015 Federal Election Results

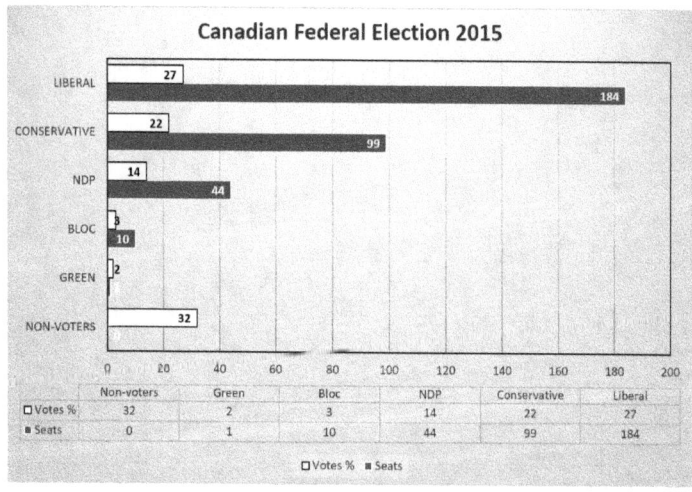

Figure 3 - 2015 Federal Election with non-voters

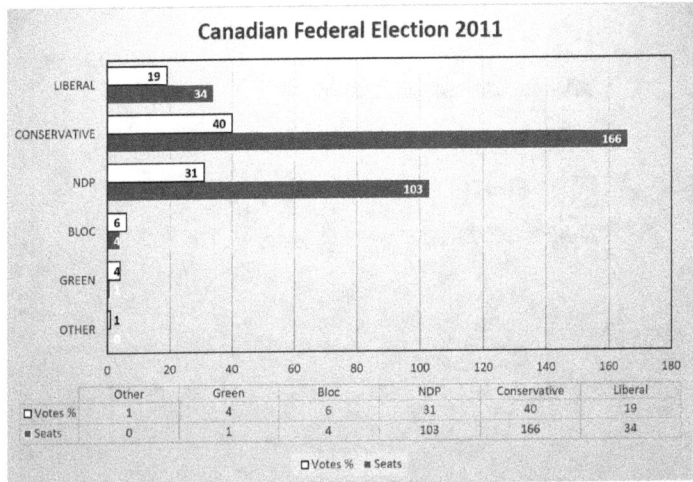

Figure 4 - 2011 Federal Election Results

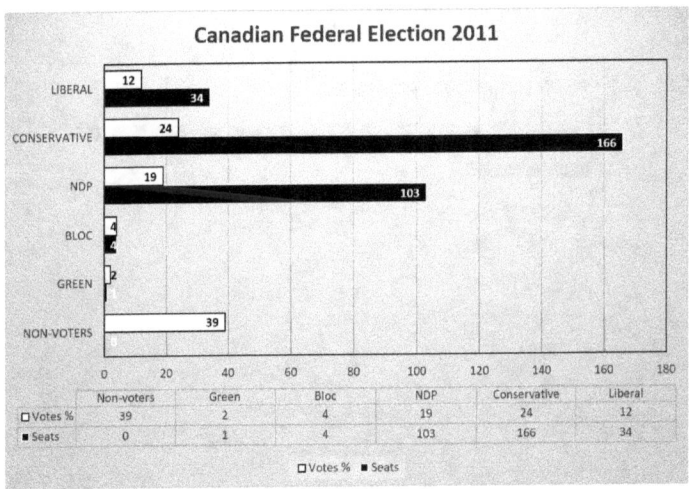

Figure 5 - 2011 Federal Election with non-voters

60   THE POWER OF YOUR VOTE

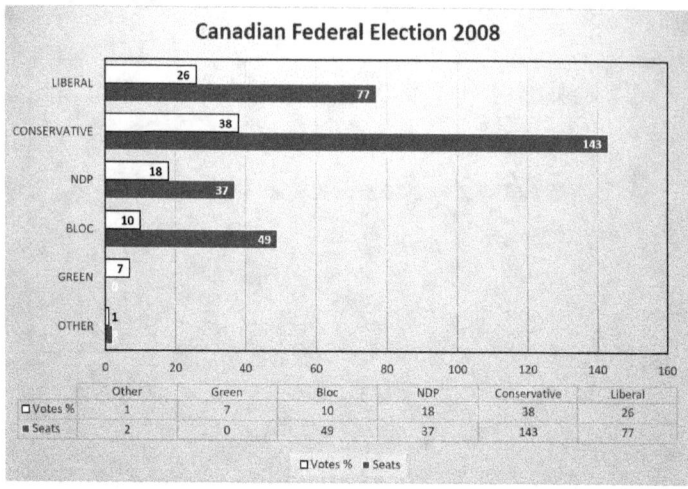

Figure 6 - 2008 Federal Election Results

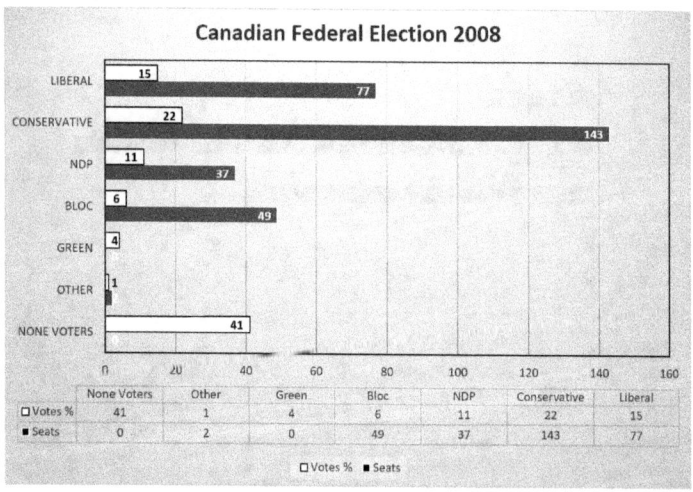

Figure 7 - 2008 Federal Election with non-voters

What is obvious is that when including the percentage of people that did not vote, the parties elected to govern either a majority or a minority government had a lesser percentage of the votes than those who did not vote. That does not make the government illegitimate. More than 50% of the voting population voted. It does put into perspective what it means to have the majority of the seats. Every single Member of Parliament had to win a majority of the votes in their riding to be elected. The hard part here is to really assess how many seats would be won by receiving these absent voters' votes.

It can be difficult to decide who to vote for. Sometimes there are no candidates you like, or each party has something you do not agree with. Some people I know say they are too busy to even follow an election or they find the debates a waste of time. What I look for is a happy medium. I give my vote to the person I trust the most to govern my country or my province for the next four years.

The voters need to take the process of elections and choice back into their own hands instead of waiting for a politician to say what they will do. The voters need to set their priorities. Voters need to ask questions directly. Voters need to start giving feedback on the politicians' behavior. Let's start the process. Let's assess and set our priorities.

PART III
YOUR PRIORITIES, YOUR PERSPECTIVES, YOUR STRATEGIES

CHAPTER 8
IT STARTS WITH YOU

No matter what is offered to us, it is important that we, the voters, decide what we want in a government. What are the priorities you want them to address in the next four years? What long term vision would you like to see for the country or your province? You will have to answer the questions, and maybe for the first time, look at government in a different way.

Each registered political party with Election Canada and each Provincial Election body will create a program to present to voters. I will not ask you to read them all. Instead, I want you to set your own priorities. This will enable you to look at an electoral program from a political party and see if their plan is compatible with your priorities. I say compatible because it may not be a perfect match, but it may be heading in the right direction.

Now if you are one of those Canadians who says you are too busy to vote, I do have a short cut for you. Everyone knows their priorities, even if they do not voice them. You have concerns when you hear a news report or see a post on Facebook. They may be informative, but they may not correspond to your perspective about government and governing. There is an online application that will take you through a series of questions. The answers are based on the different political party programs. At the end, they give you information on which party your answers align with. I do use it. It is a great tool to narrow down the political program that I will peek at and which candidates I will reach out to. At the end of this chapter, you will see the name of the application and link.

I have mentioned before the different areas of expertise that each level of government is responsible for. However, a number of areas have shared responsibilities as the Federal sends money down to the Province and the Province or Federal to municipalities. For example, if Ottawa says that they will invest in infrastructure that means money will be made available for provinces and municipalities to apply for funding for Provincial or Municipal infrastructure projects. A good example of this is public transit. Often municipalities will propose a project and request funding from both Federal and Provincial government.

Below you will find a list of possible priorities. Please add to it if I have missed something. You can go to the book's website to download a PDF version of this list so you can write down and update the list for each election. Think about the type of needs you have in the different area mentioned below, then assign it a priority level. This priority level is a good way to compare your highest priorities with the political party's program established priorities.

For example, in the area of health care, your need could be finding a family doctor, and the priority may be high because you are starting a family, or you just moved to a new location too far from your previous family doctor.

Area	Type of needs	Priority level	Political Party
Health care			
Education			
Transportation			
Environment			
Immigration			
Sports			
Arts			
Language			
Media			
Business			
Agriculture/Farming			
Fisheries/Ocean			
Employment			
Taxes and Finance			
Energy			
Infrastructures			
Defense/Rescue			
Food and water access			

After you have your priorities list, an easy way to see what party you are closes to is to use the Compass application on the CBC website (http://votecompass.com/).

CHAPTER 9
INTERVIEWING THE CANDIDATES

It is great that parties and candidates send information our way; however, it is important to remember that a campaign is really a job interview. Before giving someone your vote for the job of MP, MPP, or mayor, interview them. Now you may not be able to do one-on-one interviews with all the candidates in your riding. There is a way to use what has been published to get some answers. You can also send questions via email, social media, or at local debates.

After you have your list of priorities and used the compass application, the list of political parties that meet your needs should be much smaller. This helps you narrow down the electoral programs you may want to investigate before formulating your questions for the candidates in your riding. You can find the website of each political party on Election Canada's website. If you are pressed for time and feel that reading the programs would not help, you can still create questions from your list of priorities or what you have already heard about the different parties' promises.

When any of us go for an interview, we have to submit our résumé and answer question so the employer can assess if we are a good fit for the position. The employer may ask you what you know about the company. Every candidate in every election is applying for a job. It is a job that comes with a four year mandate, no probation period, and one review of their performance every four years.

A normal election consists of a candidate telling voters some information they deem necessary. This is the time to personally reach out to the candidates and ask our own questions. Even ask for their résumé! Yes, their résumé. Their résumé will tell you their job history and may contain some of their social engagements. If it does not contain their community engagement and service record, feel free to ask for it. You can also ask them how long they have lived in the region they are asking to represent. Sometimes, political parties can "parachute" a candidate. This can happen when a high-profile individual is asked to represent the political party. Even if they are not from the area, they might still do a good job, but it would be interesting to know what they know about the region, nonetheless.

When you create your interview email, make sure you are respectful, polite, and honest. Don't be afraid to say why you are asking for their résumé, past engagements, and affiliations. Elections are a great time to remind candidates and seasoned politicians that ultimately it is the voters that give them the power to govern. Each candidate deserves our respect. It is an investment on their part to become a candidate. Your agenda and goal of the interview email is to gain information to make a choice. By being respectful, you will have a greater chance of gaining valuable information.

It is true that there are no guarantees that the candidate will answer your interview email. That can be a factor in choosing who to vote for. You can certainly send your interview email to all the candidates in your riding and see who answers. Candidates may not be used to receiving interview emails. Give them a deadline by which you would like a response. Be realistic. Give them two to four weeks, depending on the length of the election campaign.

You can prepare your email even before the election campaign is started. Federal elections are held every four years at specific dates. This will be different if we have previously elected a minority government. Minority governments can be defeated in parliament if they face a vote of non-confidence. You can also keep notes in between elections about questions you feel need to be answered before you would give someone your vote.

I cannot guarantee that they will answer. They may even be taken aback by these requests and may simply send you a form email response with slogans. They may simply repeat party rhetoric or maybe even display some theatrics. Don't be discourage by that. Most candidates and party leaders also have social media accounts. Reach out! Social media is a great way to see how the candidates presents themselves to the public. It is called *Social* media! *Be social.* Ask them questions, reach out, respond to their post, and see what and how they answer you, or if they answer you. Again, be polite, respectful, and honest.

The same can be done for the party leaders. It may happen that you do not like the candidate in your riding based on their résumé, community track record, or how they answered your request for information. However, you might really agree with the party's program. Reach out to the party leader. And yes, you can ask them for their résumé as well. The party leader is applying for the job of Prime Minister or Premier. You as a voter have the right to know who you are electing to the top job in the country or province.

For party leaders, you will also have access to different interviews and debate performance to gain information about who they are and what they stand for. There is a possibility that party leaders are not the ones answering their emails. Every political party and third parties have communication teams. Party leaders could have a personal assistant that takes care of Twitter, Facebook, Instagram, and emails. Don't let that discourage you from reaching out. If someone wants to be a politician, they are applying for a civil servant job, therefore they are asking to work for you!

If you want ideas on what to ask candidates, start by asking the questions you feel are not being asked by the journalists. You can even use questions you heard journalists ask the leaders of the different political parties. The important thing here is to ask the questions you feel will get you the information *you need* to make an educated choice.

CHAPTER 10
PROMISES, PROMISES

Political parties and candidates like to make promises by pledging investment, tax reductions, or policy changes. They would promise us the moon if it gets them elected. It is a voter's homework to take the promises and understand their impact as best they can. It is much harder to understand the impact on the rest of the country, province and different areas of daily life. When they promise tax reductions, is that really good or is there something they are not saying about the impact of less revenue for the government?

Election promises are a way for the different parties to tell voters what they plan to do if elected to govern the country or province. Election promises are also a way to attract voters from different walks of life to vote for a certain party. Promises are to be taken with a grain of salt. As much as the different political parties are planning projects and changes, once in power, they will have to contend with the reality of dealing with other countries in terms of commerce, allegiance, and those who share our borders. As much as the Federal government can steer Canada's economy and social policies, they cannot influence what other countries do that will impact our economy.

What is important for voters is to listen to the plan of action. Some political candidates only focus on saying what other political parties will do and how that will affect you. They are probably using scare tactics to make you afraid of voting for a particular political party. Be aware of their methods; there is something wrong if they warn you about others but neglect to mention their plans. I stop listening when people use scare tactics. I stop listening when they only talk about the harmful things others will do. I do listen when they talk about their action plan because I can then comprehend their priorities and I can see if they match my own.

I really would like to see a revolution when it comes to promises. I would like to have the candidates and the political parties actually talk about their plans and how they will go about implementing them. I'm interested in knowing how their plans will affect different section of the society and how it will affect government services. I'm especially interested in why it is the best long-term plan. Often, promises are very short term mainly because each term is only four years with no guarantee to be elected for a second four year term. The hard part for voters is to see what the short-term promises mean in long term impact. I do rely on the traditional media to give me further insight into the effects of the different political promises from each party. I also look at what the third parties are saying, but again, if they try to simply scare me, I do not listen.

Yes, there are risks to certain political promises. To me, there is a great risk when someone does not speak of their own intentions and just tries to make the other parties the boogeyman. You can also just go straight to a political party website where their programs are posted and see what it says. The program should have more detail and reasoning than a 30 second commercial. It will also dispel what other political parties or third parties say about the program. Remember, it is important to have multiple sources. For political programs, it is important to go to the source itself. Remember that the program was voted for by party members and the party executive. I often wonder how the party member influences the members of parliament that answer should be in the party's program and policies.

Promises should include consequences and benefits. Promises need to be put into context to see if they are realistic. I include those questions as part of my letters to the candidates and my social interactions. When I interact with a candidate, political party, or a political party leader about electoral promises, I ask for the warnings, benefits, context, and impact of their promises. The answer I get will help me decide for whom I will vote.

Questions:

- Who benefits from the promise in the short term? In the long term?
- What are the cuts that will results from the promise being fulfilled?
- Is there missing information about what the realised promise will mean for me and my community?
- What is the impact on the most vulnerable?
- What is the impact on the environment and wildlife?
- What promise is missing from the political programs?
- What are the economic and social impact of implementing the party's program?
- Where is the money coming from to realise the promises?
- Do any programs answer my list of priorities?

CHAPTER 11
LET THE DEBATE BEGIN

A debate is normally when two teams are given a subject to debate for and against, and at the end, the judges determine who had the best arguments and who pleaded their case the best. A political debate is not the same, though each of the political party leaders will argue in favour of their political program and agenda. They will also argue against political party leaders, past accomplishments or errors, and the flaws of the other parties' programs.

Before you watch the debate, take a moment to write some notes down about the following:

- What is your bias about each of the leaders of the political parties that will be part of the debate (before it even starts)?
- What is your agenda for watching the debate?
- What are you looking to find out in this debate?

It may not be said outright, but one of the goals of the political debate is to trip the other leaders in hopes of making them look bad. That means a good portion of their answers or speeches will be spent talking badly about their opponent and not discussing their platform and plan. Most of the time, the current Prime Minister or Premier (of a province) will be the one all other leaders will attack, unless they are not leading in the polls. In that situation, attacks will be directed to the leader of the party who is ahead in the poll. Yes, again, it is important to remember that they are applying for the job to lead a country or a province. So watch their behaviour, how they interact with the others, and the words they choose.

Journalists will ask questions, some of which come from the everyday voters. Sometimes the question will be directed at one leader. The other leaders will have a chance for a rebuttal or to challenge the answer from that party leader.

Things to consider while you watch the debates: be attentive to the theatrics! Remember that each leader practices and choses arguments and words. They research their opponent and prepare their speeches. They polished their slogans and counter attacks. As much as leaders are trying to gain votes, they also need to keep their voters' base happy, like party members. This will give limits to what they can say, should say, and would say. The party leaders know everyone will study their performance and analyze everything they do or do not say. Even so, see if you notice a moment of surprise, someone who is caught off guard, or a moment of confidence and assurance.

The rhetoric leaders will use in their arguments and statements may contain unrelated facts to try to make a point or confuse the situation. These usually go through the medium of emotion. They will pair facts that will produce a strong reaction from the audience. After the initial impact of the statement, take the time to assess the facts. You may be able to see where they are mixing facts by creating a relationship of cause and effect. They may link two issues, which do not affect one another but are viewed as problems that need to be resolved. Political leaders will indirectly count on the public lack of political memory. They may even refute a previous act, mainly because the majority of voters will not know or remember what had happened at the parliament a few years back.

Every voter has an opinion of what is acceptable for a politician to say, do, or how to behave. But then again, some voters are invested in a political party like sports fan with their favorite team. This vested interest in having one political party win at all cost means they are willing to turn a blind eye from time to time on how political leader behave. That is if it gets the party to the coveted victory. Every leader comes to the debate with a strategy and an agenda. At the very least, they will want to sell their program, sell themselves, and make the least amount of mistakes possible.

It can be hard at times to watch the whole debate if theatrics and rhetoric is all that is on display. However, I suggest watching it twice. This allows you to take the time to listen to how the leaders express themselves; how they behave towards other leaders and towards the journalists. If you do not have a way to tape the debate, there should be some way to find parts, if not the entire debate, on the internet. Media outlets will replay some of the "highlights" of the debate.

The second view also helps to see through the medium of emotion. Leaders will choose key words to repeat and emphasis. If you can try to find the pattern, this will help you better understand each candidate and their party's agenda. Are they looking to make you angry at someone or some policy? Are they working so hard at making you feel a specific feeling that they make you forget they never answered the question or told what they plan to do? Are they deflecting and pointing a finger at someone else's policy, promise, or program?

It is normal for leaders to poke holes into other political party programs. However, one can do so without using adjectives that leaves the audiences with a bad taste in their mouth. It can also be done without inciting negative feeling towards government and democratic elections.

Let's bring back the ideas of bias and agenda.

Take the time to clearly understand each party leader's agenda during the debate. Using that agenda, try to identify their bias and their party's bias.

Identify the propaganda used during the debate. Notice a phrase or argument they repeated over and over. This can be especially obvious in their opening and closing statements. These are words or sentences used to push their bias and agenda.

You can go through this exercise for each candidate or simply for the ones you are thinking of voting for. In the end, you will know something you did not know. Hopefully that will help you make your choice.

PART IV
CHOICES AND VOTING

CHAPTER 12
MAKING A CHOICE

Sometimes it is hard to find that perfect candidate to give your vote and power to. It is important to consider your local candidate and how that translate to a party to put in power for the next four years. A candidate should be able to defend local needs and wants; however, we must remember that they are also part of a party. That party answers not only to all voters but to party members and what is call the party base or faithful's. There are also donors that want some of the attention.

Think of voting as your follow through from all your other civic actions and engagements. You may be very engaged in your community with volunteering and other activities. You may be very active with signing petitions, protest marches, and engaging in conversation with your MP or MPP. That is awesome! Please keep doing it. Now, follow through. Vote for the person that matches as much as possible your priorities and where you want government to put tax payer money. Voting is showing the politicians that not only will you tell them what you think throughout their mandate, you will follow through and vote for what you want your government to do.

At times, protest marches and petition can definitely get the attentions of politicians and policy makers. Voting is when voters give the power to govern. This is when politicians need you the most. Once they are elected, they are good for four years, unless they chose to step down. If a minority government is elected, they are not guaranteed a four year term as the majority of the seats are with the opposition. Usually, if the opposition feels the government is not heading in the right direction for the people who voted for them, they will introduce a vote of no-confidence and a new election will be called.

CHAPTER 13
VOTING TIME!

The hard work has been done. You have made a choice - now make it count by casting your vote. There are multiple chances to vote as there is advance polling and the day of the election to go and exercise your right to vote.

You should have received a voter's card from Election Canada. If you have not, contact Election Canada and they will help you with making sure you are on the voters list for your riding.

Your vote can be cast on the day of the election or by anticipation. There are usually multiple dates for the vote by anticipation. This information is on the voter's card. You can also find the information on the Election Canada website. The vote by anticipation is offered so that if you are going to be out of town or unable to go to the poll on Election Day, you can still vote. This can be practical for students away at college or university. Though students at colleges and universities can also vote in those local ridings, they just need to register to vote in that riding. Contact Election Canada to find out how!

When you are facing your ballot to vote, take your time to read it so that you find the person you want to vote for and follow the instructions. If you have any questions, the people at the polling station will be able to answer your questions. I have to say that I am always nervous and excited when I go vote. I take it seriously and I always make sure I vote. I have even changed my mind right there in the voting booth and other times I know exactly who I am going to vote for, without a doubt. I have also voted against a party instead of for a specific program and policies. I always have a reason to vote. I cherish the duty to elect a government. It is a part of democracy. It is essential. I respect my right to give the power to govern to an array of people that will be responsible to spend my tax dollars. They will create policies that will provide equality to all who live in my province and all of Canada. The power to govern also gives the power to decide to go to war. It gives the authority to put an emphasis on the environment, or to ensure that all Canadians get the health care they need. The elected government is also responsible for trade and relations with other countries, allies and neighbors.

The elected government cannot control the worlds' economy, nor does it have power over what other countries will or will not do for an array of political areas. However, you and I can elect a government that will take specific positions towards the world which will protect and help grow our country's quality of life.

You have reasons to vote. Vote to elect a government that will reflect your priorities and where you want the country and province to be in the next four years, and in the next 10, 15, or 20 years.

AFTERWORD
DEMOCRACY STARTS WITH A VOTE BUT DOES NOT END THERE

Democracy does not stop after an election is done and all the votes are counted. You can keep your government accountable for the next four years by communicating with your Member of Parliament. This will keep them in check as well. Continue to write to the Prime Minister or the Premier of your province. It is important to remind elected officials that not everyone voted for them. To let them know that even if they got your vote this time, it is not a guarantee of your vote at the next election.

Keep track of what the government is doing. When you hear something with which you do not agree, contact your member of parliament at the Federal and Provincial level. If they do something right, you can contact them as well. More of us need to have a conversation with elected politicians. It feels like the distance between voters and politician is a great divide. If you communicate with them, the distance will shrink. You will feel more engaged with them, and they will know how you think about their performance. Being an MP or MPP, Prime Minister or Premier is a job. Don't be afraid to assess their job performance. Journalists and third party organisations, like Green Peace or unions, often grade the accomplishment of our government based on their agenda, bias, and priorities.

Not only that, have a conversation with the media. If you had started conversions with journalist about their coverage or what they did not cover, keep it up. These journalists are still working on the news when there is no election. We can talk to the journalists. We can talk to our elected officials. We can talk to each other about our priorities, our perceptions, and opinions. We can learn from one another so that we can gain a more all-encompassing perspective.

The idea is to grow more and more comfortable with talking about political issues, policies, and government. There is bound to be a variety of perception from one day to the next about the impact of the Federal and Provincial governments' actions, policies, spending, and budget cuts. It is also important to have the media and politician learn how to give us all the information we need to better understand why decisions are made. This will ensure that we, the voters, can better understand the parties' political program and how it matches their actions. It would help accurately assess the electoral promises in a political party electoral program.

Remember that political parties, candidates of that party, and party members actively seek donations from voters. These donations don't necessarily involve a guaranteed return, like a return on investment. However, there have been reports in different newspapers and media about how sometimes it looks like the fundraising was "cash-for-access" (Annett and Thanh Ha 2017). Federal and Provincial donation limit varies at the Federal level "Political actors must disclose the names of anyone who donates more than $200." (Jansen 2016) The Financial Post has built a database entitled "Follow The Money" (Schwartz 2017) so you can check for yourself who donates to what party at the Federal and Provincial level. It is not easy information to follow. However, if you have a suspicion and you would like to check, please do.

As part of your journey in democracy, you may decide to become a member of a political party or become involved in the creation of political programs, party rules, and regulations. You can choose to keep your vote available to other parties no matter your membership. You can vote like a sports fan - no matter what your favorite party says or does, you keep voting for them. Either way, it is your choice. The power to vote is in your hands, always. If you want to know more about voters turnout, go to the Election governing bodies (see chapter 5); you can see the different percentages to understand which political party got the majority of the votes.

You can also choose to stay a free agent with no team allegiance. That is perfectly okay. Keep engaging with the different political parties. Reach out to your member of parliament, especially if you did not vote for them. Once elected, they represent you no matter their party affiliation. Reminding elected official that they do serve all their constituents first, before their political party, is a role voters should claim when honoring democracy. Otherwise, elected officials may forget who pays their salaries and who gave them the job in the first place.

Be involved in democracy. Follow through. Use the power of your vote!

REFERENCES

Annett, Evan, et Tu Thanh Ha. 2017. *Political Donation in Canada a guide.* 12 November. Accessed June 24, 2019. https://www.theglobeandmail.com/news/politics/political-donations-in-canada-a-guide/article34296694/.

BBC. 2017. *Fake Obama created using AI Tool to make phoney speeches.* 17 July. Accessed June 23, 2019. https://www.bbc.com/news/av/technology-40598465/fake-obama-created-using-ai-tool-to-make-phoney-speeches.

Chase, Steven. 2018. *Trudeau says ending Saudi Arms deal carries $1-billion price tag.* 23 October. Accessed June 23, 2019. https://www.theglobeandmail.com/politics/article-cancelling-armoured-vehicle-sale-to-saudi-arabia-could-cost-up-to/.

CRTC. 2019. *Home-Accueil.* 19 June. Accessed June 23, 2019. https://crtc.gc.ca/eng/home-accueil.htm.

Election Canada. 2019. *Information on Third Parties and Election Advertising.* 14 June. Accessed June 23, 2019. https://www.elections.ca/content.aspx?section=pol&dir=thi&document=info&lang=e.

—. 2019. *Our mission, mandate, values.* June 16. Accessed June 23, 2019. https://www.elections.ca/content.aspx?section=abo&dir=mis&document=index&lang=e.

—. 2019. *Registered Political Parties and Parties Eligible for Registration.* 14 June. Accessed June 23, 2019. https://www.elections.ca/content.aspx?section=pol&dir=par&document=index&lang=e.

—. 2019. *Voter Turnout at Federal Elections and Referendums.* 23 05. Accessed 06 23, 2019. https://www.elections.ca/content.aspx?section=ele&dir=turn&document=index&lang=e.

Fraser Institute. 2014. *Cancelling Contrats: The Power of Governments to Unilaterally Alter Agreements.* 22 October. Accessed June 23, 2019. https://www.fraserinstitute.org/research/cancelling-contracts-power-governments-unilaterally-alter-agreements.

Jansen, Harold. 2016. *Financing in Canada.* 14 December. Accessed June 24, 2019. https://

www.thecanadianencyclopedia.ca/en/article/party-financing.

Laughey, Dan. 2007. *Key Themes in Media Theory*. Berkshire: The McGRAW-Hill Companies.

O'Sullivan, Donie. 2019. *Pentagons race against deepfakes*. January. Accessed June 23, 2019. https://www.cnn.com/interactive/2019/01/business/pentagons-race-against-deepfakes/.

Schwartz, Zane. 2017. *Follow the Money*. Accessed June 24, 2019. http://special.nationalpost.com/follow-the-money/feature.

Statistics Canada. 2019. *Labour force characteristics by province, monthly, seasonnally adjusted.* 23 June. Accessed June 23, 2019. https://www150.statcan.gc.ca/t1/tbl1/en/tv.action?pid=1410028703&pickMembers%5B0%5D=3.1&pickMembers%5B1%5D=4.1.

Taulli, Tom. 2019. *Deepfake: What you need to know.* 15 June. Accessed June 23, 2019. https://www.forbes.com/sites/tomtaulli/2019/06/15/deepfake-what-you-need-to-know/#5fb21455704d.

The Canada Guide. 2017. *Past Canadian Federal Election Results.* 21 April. Accessed June 23, 2019. http://www.thecanadaguide.com/data/federal-elections/.

The Canadian Press. 2018. *Cancelling Saudi Arabia arms deal would cost $1 billion: Trudeau.* 23 October. Accessed June 23, 2019.

https://edmonton.citynews.ca/2018/10/23/cancelling-saudi-arabia-arms-deal-would-cost-1-billion-trudeau/.

Urback, Robyn. 2018. *Canada can't afford to cancel the Saudi arms deal - and the Trudeau government knows it.* 30 November. Accessed June 23, 2019. https://www.cbc.ca/news/opinion/saudi-arms-deal-1.4926484.

Vincent, James. 2017. *New AI research makes it easier to create fake footage of someone speaking.* 12 July. Accessed June 23, 2019. https://www.theverge.com/2017/7/12/15957844/ai-fake-video-audio-speech-obama.

INDEX

A

accountability, 3
accountable, 3, 89
action, 2, 15, 21, 26, 73, 95
active, 3, 83
ads, 2
advertisement, 26
advocate, 9
agenda, 3, 7, 8, 11, 12, 13, 15, 16, 18, 20, 26, 41, 43, 53, 69, 76, 78, 79, 90
AI, xiii, 53, 93, 96
airways, 40
angle, 38
Artificial Intelligence, xiii, 53
audience, 8, 11, 18, 25, 26, 78, 105

B

background, 40
ballot, 1, 3, 86
beliefs, 4, 12, 14, 19, 39, 53
beneficial, 15, 40, 50
benefits, 8, 74, 75
bias, 7, 8, 11, 12, 14, 15, 16, 17, 20, 40, 41, 43, 76, 79, 90
Bias, 11, 13, 14, 18
biases, 13, 14
Biases, 13
blind spots, 14
blogs, vi, 42
Brian Mulroney, 1
broad, 8
broadcast, 26, 41, 43
budget, 42, 54, 90
built, 11, 43, 91
bureaucracy, 51

C

campaign, 1, 2, 3, 14, 15, 20, 27, 40, 41, 68, 70
campaigns, 4, 9, 27, 33, 49
Campaigns, 2
Canada, xiii, xiv, 1, 2, 3, 8, 9, 10, 13, 28, 33, 34, 35, 39, 40, 41, 47, 48, 49, 53, 65, 68, 73, 85, 86, 93, 94, 95, 96
Canadian, vii, xiii, 28, 33, 41, 49, 50, 95
candidate, 2, 3, 4, 12, 13, 14, 19, 27, 28, 34, 40, 41, 44, 45, 53, 54, 69, 70, 71, 74, 79, 83
candidates, 2, 4, 11, 13, 14, 22, 26, 27, 29, 33, 34, 37, 39, 40, 41, 44, 45, 46, 50, 53, 61, 66, 68, 69, 70, 72, 73, 74, 90, 105
Capitalism, 8
capitalist, 8
centre, 8, 9
challenge, 55, 77
change, 3, 4, 16, 22, 25, 38, 45, 47, 48, 50, 51, 52, 54, 55
channels, 39, 41
charged, 15, 16, 21, 27, 45
choice, 2, 3, 4, 10, 12, 28, 61, 70, 71, 79, 83, 85, 91
chose, 11, 84, 105
citizen, 1, 33
citizens, vii, 3, 4, 52
clean, 2, 27
climate, 55
commercial, 15, 17, 20, 26, 29, 40, 74
commercials, 2, 9, 12, 15, 17, 21, 26, 39, 53
common sense, 14
communication, 11, 12, 14, 18, 20, 39, 45, 71, 105
communications, 3, 15
Communism, 8
communist, 9
communities, 42, 43
community, 8, 69, 71, 75, 83
concepts, 11
consequence, 26, 50
consequences, 25, 26, 55, 74
conservative parties, 8
Conservative Party, xiv, 8
consumers, 47, 48
content, vi, 7, 14, 16, 20, 43, 44, 72, 94
context, 2, 11, 53, 74
corporations, 8
corrections, 45
country, 1, 3, 4, 9, 13, 24, 44, 51, 52, 56, 61, 65, 71, 72, 77, 86, 87
Crown Corporations, 8
CRTC, xiii, 41, 94

D

damaging, 54
debate, 4, 15, 17, 26, 29, 55, 71, 76, 77, 78, 79
debates, 12, 39, 41, 61, 68, 77

decide, 2, 3, 28, 51, 55, 61, 65, 74, 86, 91
decipher, 11
decision, 4, 27, 52
definition, 11
democracy, vii, 3, 17, 86, 91, 92
democratic, vii, 34, 79
destruction, 54
development, 9, 22, 40
Dictionaries, 11
dictionary, 11, 16
dirty, 2, 27
discourse, 14
discussions, 17
distortion, 13, 19, 26
distortions, 20, 21
division, 26

E

economic, 9, 22, 50, 75
economy, 20, 48, 54, 55, 73, 86
educated, i, v, 12, 46, 71
education, 2, 47
elected, 2, 3, 4, 12, 28, 34, 39, 49, 50, 51, 52, 54, 61, 70, 72, 73, 84, 86, 89, 90, 91
elected officials, 52, 89, 90
election, 1, 2, 3, 4, 9, 10, 12, 20, 21, 28, 33, 34, 35, 37, 39, 40, 45, 50, 54, 56, 61, 66, 69, 70, 84, 85, 89, 90, 105
Election Canada, 33, 34, 35, 40, 85, 86
Election Day, 3, 27, 85

elections, vii, 1, 9, 33, 34, 35, 36, 37, 44, 53, 56, 61, 70, 79, 94, 95, 105
Elections, 1, 33, 45, 69, 94
electronic, vi, 44
emotional, 15, 26, 27, 29
emotionally, 15, 16, 21, 27, 45
emotions, 2, 15, 16, 20, 25, 26, 27, 28
Emotions, 25, 26, 29
environment, 2, 9, 20, 22, 54, 55, 75, 86
ethics, 2, 52
examples, 12
exclusion, 14
executive, 40, 74
experiences, 12, 13, 19, 21, 105
expert, 19, 43, 54
extreme, 8, 10, 14, 54
extremes, 8

F

Facebook, 34, 42, 44, 66, 71
fact, 2, 21, 43
facts, 2, 15, 16, 19, 25, 26, 27, 50, 77
fake, 43, 53, 93, 96
Federal, vi, xiv, 1, 4, 8, 13, 24, 28, 33, 34, 35, 37, 39, 42, 46, 47, 48, 50, 52, 56, 58, 59, 60, 66, 70, 73, 89, 90, 91, 94, 95
focus, 10, 14, 16, 20, 23, 45, 73
four, 2, 4, 20, 22, 28, 49, 54, 56, 61, 65, 69, 70, 73, 83, 84, 87, 89, 105

G

gatekeepers, 41, 42
goal, 11, 12, 15, 27, 69
goals, 12, 27, 77
govern, 1, 2, 12, 13, 26, 29, 39, 49, 50, 51, 52, 61, 69, 72, 84, 86
governing, 39, 46, 50, 54, 56, 66, 91
government, 2, 3, 8, 9, 10, 20, 22, 23, 24, 27, 28, 33, 47, 48, 49, 50, 51, 52, 54, 55, 61, 65, 66, 70, 72, 73, 79, 83, 84, 86, 87, 89, 90, 96
Government, 8, 28, 54
governments, 4, 9, 23, 28, 48, 49, 70, 90, 94
Governments, 3, 54, 94
Green Party, xiii, 9

H

health care, 2, 8, 67, 86
healthy, 55

I

idea, 9, 10, 90
ideas, 13, 14, 38, 44, 52, 71, 79
ideology, 14
impact, 48, 55, 72, 73, 74, 75, 78, 90
impression, 20
income, 47, 48
Individuals, 8
influence, 2, 8, 11, 13, 14, 15, 16, 39, 43, 45, 73
influenced, 11
inform, 18, 28, 38
information, vi, 13, 14, 15, 16, 19, 20, 23, 26, 27, 33, 34, 35, 37, 38, 39, 40, 41, 42, 43, 44, 46, 49, 50, 51, 52, 53, 55, 66, 68, 69, 70, 71, 75, 85, 90, 91
Information, 38, 94
informed, 3, 28, 29, 39
Instagram, 34, 42, 44, 71
intentions, 26, 74
internet, 9, 34, 41, 42, 44, 46, 52, 53, 78
interpret, 4
interpretation, 12
interview, 4, 15, 40, 68, 69, 70
interviews, 12, 40, 68, 71
investment, 2, 49, 69, 72, 91
issue, 18, 19, 21, 22, 26, 27, 38
issues, 2, 12, 18, 20, 21, 46, 78, 90

J

job, 3, 20, 27, 49, 52, 68, 69, 71, 77, 90, 92
jobs, 2
journalist, 23, 42, 43, 90
judgement, 26
judgements, 45

L

leader, 2, 13, 19, 35, 50, 71, 74, 77, 78, 79
leaders, 13, 20, 24, 40, 44, 50, 70, 71, 76, 77, 78, 79
left, 8, 9, 10, 22, 28, 41
legacy, 51
legislation, 52, 54
level of government, 47, 48
Liberal Party, 8
lobbyists, vii, 4, 52

M

massaged, 11
McLuhan, 25, 26
meaning, 11, 15, 16
meanings, 11, 12, 16
means, vi, 2, 11, 13, 48, 52, 55, 56, 61, 66, 77, 78
media, 2, 13, 19, 23, 26, 39, 40, 41, 42, 43, 44, 52, 53, 68, 70, 73, 90, 91
medium, 2, 21, 25, 26, 27, 28, 29, 40, 61, 78, 79
medium of emotions, 2, 21, 27, 28
member, 3, 40, 74, 89, 91, 105
Member of Parliament, xiv, 3, 45, 61, 89
membership, 2, 3, 91
message, 2, 4, 5, 7, 8, 11, 12, 14, 15, 16, 18, 19, 25, 26, 27, 28, 29, 39, 43, 44, 50, 53, 105
messages, 2, 14, 15, 16, 18, 20, 21, 25, 26, 43, 44, 53
money, vii, 40, 46, 47, 48, 55, 66, 75, 84, 95
monitor, 3, 41
MP, xiv, 3, 68, 83, 90
multiple, 16, 21, 38, 46, 55, 74, 85
Municipal, 4, 66
municipality, 1, 13
myth, 50
myths, 46

N

NAFTA, xiv, 1
narrative, 2, 42
NDP, xiv, 9
needs, 2, 4, 12, 14, 29, 34, 48, 51, 54, 66, 67, 68, 83
New Democratic Party, xiv, 9
news, 22, 39, 40, 41, 42, 55, 66, 90, 93, 96
newspaper, 26, 42, 46
newspapers, 39, 41, 91

O

old age, 8
online, 40, 43, 66
Online, 41
opinion, 18, 19, 20, 22, 24, 38, 78, 96
opinions, 18, 19, 20, 21, 22, 23, 38, 41, 42, 45, 90
opposite, 8, 38

organisations, 9, 37, 90
owners, 41, 44

P

participate, vii, 3
participation, 3
party, vii, xiii, 2, 3, 4, 8, 9, 12, 13, 14, 22, 27, 28, 35, 39, 40, 43, 44, 45, 50, 51, 53, 56, 61, 65, 66, 67, 70, 71, 72, 73, 74, 75, 76, 77, 78, 79, 83, 86, 90, 91, 95
party members, vii, 45, 50, 74, 77, 83, 90
pendulum, 8
percentage, 56, 61
perception, 14, 19, 20, 21, 22, 24, 26, 38, 90
Perception, 18, 20
perceptions, 18, 21, 22, 23, 42, 90
Perceptions, 20
perspective, 14, 18, 21, 22, 23, 26, 38, 44, 45, 61, 66, 90
Perspective, 18, 21, 22
perspectives, 38, 42, 44
persuade, 11
philosophies, 8, 9
philosophy, 7, 10
plan, 2, 28, 51, 65, 72, 73, 77, 79
platform, 3, 39, 43, 77
platforms, 39, 44
PM, xiv, 3

point of view, 2, 11, 16, 18, 21, 22
points of view, 13, 16, 21, 22, 38
policies, 22, 49, 73, 74, 86, 90
policy, vii, 20, 72, 79, 84
policy makers, vii, 84
political, 2, 3, 4, 7, 8, 9, 10, 11, 12, 13, 14, 15, 16, 17, 19, 20, 21, 22, 24, 25, 26, 27, 28, 29, 33, 35, 37, 39, 41, 43, 44, 46, 49, 50, 51, 53, 56, 65, 66, 68, 69, 71, 72, 73, 74, 75, 76, 77, 78, 79, 86, 90, 91, 93, 105
Political parties, 2, 18, 21, 23, 27, 28, 50, 53, 72
political party, 2, 3, 8, 10, 12, 14, 19, 20, 22, 24, 27, 28, 29, 35, 40, 49, 50, 51, 53, 56, 65, 66, 68, 69, 71, 73, 74, 76, 78, 79, 90, 91, 105
politician, 3, 28, 51, 52, 54, 61, 71, 78, 90
politicians, vii, 2, 4, 18, 20, 21, 24, 46, 51, 54, 56, 61, 69, 84, 89
politics, 9, 11, 17, 19, 20, 21, 22, 25, 53, 54, 93
Politics, 4
power, 1, 2, 3, 4, 12, 22, 24, 26, 27, 28, 29, 39, 45, 47, 49, 52, 53, 69, 72, 83, 84, 86, 91, 92, 94, 105
prejudice, 14

Premier, 13, 71, 77, 89, 90
Prime Minister, xiv, 3, 13, 22, 71, 77, 89, 90
priorities, i, v, 3, 4, 10, 28, 40, 61, 63, 65, 66, 67, 68, 73, 75, 83, 87, 90
process, vii, 17, 61
production, 7
program, 3, 10, 12, 27, 28, 50, 65, 66, 71, 74, 75, 76, 78, 79, 86, 90
programs, 8, 9, 14, 22, 24, 43, 44, 66, 68, 74, 75, 76, 79, 91
Progressive Conservative, xiv, 1
promises, 4, 19, 46, 69, 72, 73, 74, 75, 90
propaganda, 8, 9, 11, 14, 15, 16, 22, 25, 40, 43, 44, 79
Propaganda, 11, 15, 16, 18, 22
proposition, 40
province, xiv, 1, 3, 4, 13, 24, 35, 39, 44, 48, 51, 52, 61, 65, 71, 72, 77, 86, 87, 89, 95
Provincial, xiv, 1, 4, 13, 24, 28, 33, 35, 37, 42, 46, 47, 48, 50, 52, 56, 65, 66, 89, 90, 91
public, 2, 42, 66, 70, 78
public opinion, 2
publish, 45
publishing date, 45
purpose, 27, 44

Q

question, 45, 53, 69, 77, 79
questions, 4, 15, 19, 39, 51, 61, 65, 66, 68, 69, 70, 71, 74, 77, 86

R

radio, 39, 40, 41, 46
reaction, 15, 25, 78
reception, 7
references, 12
region, 3, 41, 44, 69
research, 9, 13, 27, 46, 55, 77, 94, 96
resources, 4, 43, 54
revenues, 47
riding, 3, 19, 44, 52, 61, 68, 70, 85, 86
right, vi, 2, 8, 9, 10, 49, 50, 52, 56, 65, 71, 84, 85, 86, 89
roads, 8

S

sales tax, 47
scapegoat, 15
schools, 8
search, 9, 53
situation, 15, 16, 21, 22, 38, 43, 45, 77, 78
situations, 14, 54
Socialism, 8
social media, 39, 42, 43, 44, 52
social status, 29
socio-capitalist, 8
solution, 3, 15, 18, 22

source, 11, 19, 38, 39, 40, 41, 42, 43, 52, 74
sources, 16, 38, 39, 42, 46, 55, 74
special interest group, 27
spectrum, 7, 8, 9, 10, 11, 16, 42
speech, 15, 19, 20, 26, 29, 39, 96
stations, 41
statistics, 15, 16, 25, 26, 27, 34, 37
stories, 41, 42, 45
strategies, 9
subject, 13, 16, 17, 18, 19, 21, 38, 43, 76
subjects, 18, 22, 45
surveys, 20
sustainable, 9
system, vi, 8

T

tax bracket, 47
tax cut, 48
taxed, 47
taxes, 8, 46, 47, 48
tax reduction, 47, 48
technology, 25, 43, 93
television, 26, 39, 41, 46
third, 9, 14, 15, 20, 22, 33, 40, 43, 71, 73, 74, 90
tools, 4, 11, 35
traditional, 39, 41, 42, 43, 53, 73
Traditional, 40, 41, 43
transit, 8, 66
tunnel vision, 21, 38

Twitter, 34, 42, 44, 71

U

unemployment, 8
United States, vi, 8

V

values, 2, 94
vision, 21, 22, 28, 55, 65
vote, vii, 1, 2, 3, 4, 11, 12, 14, 15, 26, 27, 34, 41, 51, 52, 53, 55, 56, 61, 66, 68, 70, 72, 74, 83, 84, 85, 86, 87, 89, 91, 92
voter, 2, 11, 14, 25, 27, 28, 34, 43, 56, 71, 72, 78, 85
voters, vii, 2, 3, 4, 11, 14, 22, 23, 25, 26, 27, 28, 33, 35, 37, 46, 50, 52, 53, 56, 57, 58, 59, 60, 61, 65, 69, 72, 73, 77, 78, 83, 84, 85, 89, 90, 91, 105
Voters, 3, 61
voter turnout, 34, 56
voting, 1, 3, 4, 28, 29, 51, 61, 73, 79, 83, 86, 91, 105

W

website, 10, 33, 34, 35, 39, 66, 67, 68, 74, 85
websites, vi, 9, 37, 41, 42
word, 11, 12, 15, 16, 50
words, 11, 12, 14, 16, 25, 27, 29, 53, 77, 79
Words, 11

ABOUT THE AUTHOR

Marie-Agnès Pilon is a first time author who chose to talk about elections in a way that creates communication between the voters and candidates. She went back to school to learn communication and its structure. She worked for twenty years as a programmer analyst but found her passion for language pulled her back to school. Communication theory gave her inspiration to investigate the balance between the author of the message and the audience of the message.

This book is the result of what she learned in school and her life experiences with elections. She looks forward to each election and engaging with candidates of all parties. She is not a member of any political associations, though she has signed a few petitions. She is not a donor to any political party. She truly believes in voting and choosing to bestow power to a political formation for the next four years.

www.ingramcontent.com/pod-product-compliance
Lightning Source LLC
LaVergne TN
LVHW011844060526
838200LV00054B/4160